TABULA ROSA

TABULA ROSA

Rachel Blau DuPlessis

Potes & Poets Press Inc. Elmwood, Connecticut. 1987

Acknowledgements

The poems and works in this book have appeared:

"The Poems of Sappho," "Madrigal," "Rose" and "Sister Rachel's
    Spirit Tree" in *Paper Air* 3, 1 (1982)
"Praxilla's Silliness" in *H.D.: Woman and Poet* (1986)
"Crowbar" in *Sulfur* 8 (1983)
"Killing Me" and "Eclogue" in *Sulfur* 1 (1981)
"Ode" in *Sulfur* 3 (1982)
"Megaliths" and "Selvedge" in *Montemora* 7 (1980)
"Two Gypsies" and "Moth: Ode to Psyche" as the chapbook *Gypsy/
    Moth* (Oakland: Coincidence Press, 1984)
"Oil" reprinted from *Wells* (New York: Montemora, 1980)
"Afterimage" in *Temblor* 4 (1986)

"Writing" in *Ottotole* 1 (1985); some sections reprinted in *HOW(ever)*
    2 (1985) and some sections reprinted in *Constant Red/Mingled
    Damask* (1987), Cambridge, England

"Draft #1: It" and "Draft #2: She" in *Temblor* 5 (1987)

Many thanks to these publications and to their editors.

cover design: Richard Wilkins.   ISBN 0-937013-19-6

Otherhow, for the HOW(ever)'s

Contents

I. from *The "History of Poetry"*

II. Drafts

I.   from *The "History of Poetry"*

She cannot forget the history of poetry
because it is not hers.

The Poems of Sappho

Tender pain
flat milk
a chest for holding women's things.
Under the flesh-pink moon
I keep my hand cupped.

Soft bread
fresh milk
so round and uncaring
the clear-voiced moon,
a lyre, guitar and mandolin.

I lie face down
upon a tender pillow.
Rosy-fingered, moons
two minds' desire:
to be one, to be two.

I want and yearn
but never be enough.
But dry breath and a dripping towel
made me stop;
and over my eyes dropped the dark sleep of night.

1981

Praxilla's Silliness

for none but a simpleton would put cucumbers
and the like on a par with the sun and the moon.

Zenobius, Proverbs: *Lyra Graeca,* III.

Almost
rounded moon,
Its unspilling
meniscus—

Light.

Honeyed face of the sibylline
earth.

Everything message, every randomness
twigs fallen just like that   here

bright lined bulging square.

Pepo   pepo   pepo
bird-ripe
fruit of melon, cucumber, squash, pumpi-
kin

slimy-seeded   cries   hot
August bouncing.

Sweet the push push out of the cell

mint watery by waysides
soft-leafed basil
tipped by bushy bracts

cusps of the moon.

Under the fingernails
dirt, flour, yeast

crusts of the sun.

Walk down the road until you go under it.

. .

Dew on the wheat field wells up bread.
Stars, grass, fruit, all variants

Bite down.

The light travels like salt
The dark is thirst
deep shadows
of longing for more light—

But is not the longing for shadows
brightness

earth of the meeting tides?

. .

Wood white
large white little white
littler fritillaries

wayward

"lords" of air.

Green plums red plums yellow sun
grizzled dotty (newsprint) juice
the drupy fruits

      signz
      places

always russing somewhere
A leaf's moist papery crescent sloughs off.

Of silver-waxy bloom
of cuke uncurls
I sing.

The flea lights brisk upon
one tucked foot in the dark.

Mark.

                  . .

Written veins the stones' intrusions
wander
untranslated rocks.

Me goes leaping full and empty.

Now the dead dare coming closer.

All is inscribed,
nothing feeds them,

every day a heavy vulval loaf.

Are you ready
to go down
by the water?

What cannot be said
will get wept.

We live a little patch it doth
go forward
into grief

small lilac leafed
no blossom
white feather, blossom.

. .

Travel through
picking and washing.
Flesh level, iridescent.

Roads travelled, roads untravelled
often equal.

Heavy as stone, loose as honey
earth
is constantly falling into earth.

So dress for the journey.
Pink for the cave
Pink for the endless stairwell

One hell, two deaths,
three tasteless oatcakes.

. .

What starts and calls and whistles
through the long clicking night?

Littoral, on the jot and tittle coast-
line,
plup,
that the
little tides
catch into gravel, stars.

What I miss most *when dead* is the travelling
and after, stars
the shining sun and moon

crisp cucumbers in season
the apples bright
black-seeded *pears.*

But when I am living, bite hard
into the crossroads

cukies wet and apples sweet
I can sing and I can eat.

       . .

Bury
unbury

life deciduous as the moon.

       . .
       .

1983

Madrigal

In the green wood
girls are twittering
and birds are lolling in the hamlets

their day off
today; tomorrow
it's back to the forest.

Cuccu-nu
pee-shee
pipiol
oi weh
tuwhitta woo
tereu

sound the songs
hidden in bushes.

1981

Rose

Well the green
and this its crowning
sweet the moment
common, fated
weeps the little
dripping baby.

Well the crimson's
lavish touching
clock of petals
ends by falling
black and dark
the noisy baby.

Well the rose
is filled with
roses,
well the baby
filled with people:

me none
alone
foresee
the rose.

1982

Crowbar

Snow on o-
pen
yellow for-
sythia.

'Sno
won
open force
scythe
ya.

No one
yell ow—you
yellow mortal thing
ringed in
dull earth's icy garland.

Name this wane,
this damaged foreign spring.
For swain,
who won?
Name this pain,
poem,
whosever
tune this was.

.

Prying
another impleasurable
forever re-
tardy poem
heavily up.

For all the world's sweet bolts
of fern and rose

intentional petals, leafy leaves
pressed in this paper-book
finding's clues—
trouvez!

Nose down in the field
Papery poppy "beautiful"
at the edge of wheat,

inchemeal
dumb to the marge
mere

Gleaner:
silence in between
coups.

Even the lever is a gleaning.
"Thou" art the fulcrum.

.

Cold moon's circling, half a ring-
pale smile

Ivory hand
ivory breast
ivory front
marble foot
stone stairwell

A name that means nothing
neither blessed nor laurel
no aureole no wreath

tastes the ends of dripping hair in her mouth

woman half in dream and half in waking

woman between dream and waking
weeping on both sides of the bar-
rier

starry;   eyed.

Not on hills but "hills"
nor by water, but "water"
or from desire, but from
"desire."

Her eyes birds wings fountains
Her smile
under see.
Her hand
a peony sodden on its stem.
One leg tucked up, knee under her chin.
The other dangles,
sock rumpled, loose elastic.
She rests on her buttocks.

                    .

Frozen snow lying in shadow

my heart in the circle of a wet shadow

She is the landscape
Fountain and Mirror

for whom?
bending over the crib enveloping form?
gleaming in the moon, as breasts, as eyes.

and who
moans this drone
mimes lyric tithing?
Is it

Me

As She
or Her?

Or is me He?

Also consider for
whom am I, say, being
these eyes, these breasts?
What pulse beat for the icons

ticking off opaque cuneiform wedgies

whether I speak
about Her
or whether, being her, I can speak—
given the range of "speaking" in the first place—
at all.

Tuning the recorder,
a wider distance between fipple and body
thins the tone
but brings it into alignment
with more legitimate instruments.

What kinds and conditions of
longing   of hunger   for
whom
do I nock the arrow
for whom
wrists bound by delicate leather thongs
do I face the straw-stuffed target?

When even one telegraphic
phoneme, one-half more syllable
sibillent (s/he) you (little flirt you vixen)
close-pulled feather,

defines language and centers
what   me   they   is

(and silvery circles kiss the waiting shore).

She
is a jewel in this setting she
an emerald in the silver rain
I weep.

         .

Moreover
I would construct
a ring of green hills
cover of wildflowers' fronds
bowing under close roaring
winds

a fountain eagles
fly down to drink
river war mirror window paper

to worship
to hold her
in the center.

*For she can cast green
over any strength or disciple
of shadow.*

         .

Production of language cribbed
by (from) what decorum?

This is a spurt of brilliant
desire, not a little kiss,

juncture of pain and shaking.

A light   a wind   a green
I was, it was the world
accompanied me, as it does every
one
but it pierced
in me
my two-headed arrow.

                    .

The desire for the one seen in the mirror
the desire for one who mirrors
the desire for the mirror
the desire for being the one who mirrors
the revolt of the mirror
the sestina.

                    .

"greetings greenest branch"
ever renewing cycle of seasons
and women
who dare break
the cycle an icon
whose body
existed
nowhere understood
every-
where told, waves of sound, tune
around it is somehow
unapproachable, elegiac, that it couldn't
ever be voided if I
chose another
fold to un word
the disturbance (a person)
it made

claiming (lov'd) my
green my brown my red my creamy, moony
white.

Hart
hurt in the heart o dear.

Bitter desire, un-
and willing-
to-will desire

one line of the ankle touch
sock dangles the desire
sullen, being
what I
woman am
said (what else?) to be.
My breasts my eyes enfolding mine.
And am; I am.

So kneel scribe, eye, bird
crescent kneeler bird
in the feather breath,
greetings.

It is impossible,
love, to love
and impossible to unlove

green shapes of fair women.

.

Being or having been
"a" woman
thru which a man en-
tered "be"

yond lang
wedge,
edged the unutterable
exactly: that dance.

Rumba samba
"papa love mambo"
fulsome agendas, rigid agents,
everywhere
entered unutterable
appropriative humility
hey what
luxury
of the one situation with many
palpable gateways

Uhh yeah.

Marimbas repeating rhythms
organizations of blackness:
lust in awe
cruel the twirling, dipping rhymes

those shake-it couples.

.

How do I want you?
"like" a pilgrimage starting out
despite a flooded roadway
"like" a car sharp in reverse, a gravel
driveway
"like" what?

In all splendor in all the
pulse and blah the strain it comes
it never stoppeth

bearded iris
veined with a "bruised" color
dreamy against a white lace powerless.

Rush from those arms
rush to those arms
there "I" am is it certain
I am there?

Being the sibyllent secret stream inside fountain
endless pulsing of fountains   cool feathers

their cycles

translucent fear
on the bright angel trail.

Try mud sky, lunar eclipse, that rare.

Low red belly of the moon h-

ung

hunger of the sky.

                    .

Stretched out on the horizon
every mound of woman
a mound of earth
clay
she swallowed
searching any nourishment
from her unutterable hollows.

Hey ho Bonibell,
cannibal.

                    .

Women walk by abstractedly
with glass in their pockets.

We look dumb, they think
but are not dumb.

Words of natives whirr around them.
That we were once here,

weathered glass
some sharp slivers mirrors they finger

sleep, pain, desire
and again desire

that wanderer,
but are not here now.

               .

My shadow flickers black
over lady-green shadow.
Travelling many direction'd crossings
head blank
gridded with ever tunefulest song

one compromised means of transport
limp
foot   who can say "I" or "I'd" it is all
practically not-I
another fusion
cells annealed   the nucleus of a Lady
in some woman drags
herself long thirsty
and heavy-thighed
up to the Fountain or any ego-ideal
like that.

               .

'Tis
Poem:

that around
its words

it's Words.

The silver ring she threw away
ringed by the fountain's silver
ring.

         .

End of the dogwood
start of the greenwood
end of the greenword song
but time repeats its greens and browns
the clues it leaves declare.

     lay dee   hist! story
     l'idée   mystery
     lay dés   My hyster   y

who threw a ring who kept a ring
who caroled the rich greenwoody song
all MherY duplicity of gesture
a throw of the ring not
abolishing

the Nymph of the Fountain:
to pray the nymph for this her safe return
to stop up the crevices of the mountain
a little IUD of wire this nymph n-
ode   cannot stand it, inseparable
complicit and disgusted desire.

A crowbar of trobar

pow
it
tries
desire, "thou"
the fulcrum

pries open the cellular troping
nucleii and the ever
drowning dark abyss

My Lady   Me Lady.

                    .

La la lie
laura lie
don't lie
some
love
the fame of the place
this singing hole its reason.

Wreathe thru the "bowels of the earth"
springtime's sibillent whispers
you (thou) can(st)
still today get draped and happy wear
the green gossamer of nature
down derry down.

What stories
no end to these stories
the diaries have dearies
the stories starry
a derry
down a thickening
o.

Prying them up

out of the self—
unpicking atoms with a cigarillo.

Lay dee
dear hood ship sheathe
in the wild wift wood
whose feet slog sullen
over the gnarly ground of gnosis,

if ever.

.

Precious poetry? ha!
Rage of being
the impossible self.

Rupture
the reverberating lyric cell by cell
edge of the tree-green strips'
deciduous space

the stretched pulse of number
singing in my heart.

Beauty red and beauty white
green site brown site
gapping along like shadows in the
wilderness from
objects
dappled away.

Porous breathing stone
like lace worn thin by seepage:
woman like what? poem like what?
complicit with the repetoire
ambivalent to the repetoire
Lady Cloudy Mountain

cloudy clutter mountains
struggle with the white atmospheres
of yearning   such limpid mountings
fix the figures
milky mouth on mine.

.

The gnotty pond
some blue black coil caved deep in mountain's lime
and poem's lava.
Waters pooling from sets of high country valleys
tro- and trickling thru patterned singers of passage
-bar no one
source of mille
phasia dribbles big libble
wa-
the intent pooling
o -tears
meniscus filling past its lim-
it breaking under selves' multiple
leveled sinters;

Stone secreted path
dispersong the
Gouffre

in mar-
row phasal cluster's
pearly

Surge.

Leafy crevices. White foam.
Nacreous
re-immersion blank
remission;
rivulets that rush into the body of

argument,
double crossing streams
bright-headed arrows
engorged with this ancient targeted song.

Milk of the culture's teeming

gushes at my $^{HU}_{A}$NGRY weaning.

Fontaine de Vaucluse, 1981–
Swarthmore, PA, 1983.

Killing Me

I had a dream I killed you
before death's deep doorway.

You sought to kill me
at the dream-naked doorway?

Lightly lifted sleep-laden
arms long and small

and wreathed you
sweetly,

fleeing bright heavy danger
to take bread at your hand.

Why killeth she me to get
this doorway?

Who skulks
on the pink limen of the dawnway?

No murder:
I am worth your killing;

I would kill myself
to stand at the threshold

under the lintel
naked foot stalking

on the packed ground of this place
the clay ground of this thresher's place

AND beat the hard bread grains
burst from the baskety grasses.

1981

Eclogue

Gave me the milk
curdling
sour-soft scum naked
water light and
glittering where I am
folded roads.

Gave the bread
honeyed, gold
fulls
the woolly
cells of yeast.

Mouth to the earth
takes earth,
to water,
water

mouth to the green
eats
top and tuft and danky dirt

mouth to the wet bud pool
drinks hard

kissing the fallen leaves aside
o'er green fat hills
heart
snaked
round the pearly
membrane of day,
O honey hills a hole a spring.

Heigh ho silly
sheep. Leap!

onto the green and moody
pastures
over the green and seedy
grasses

that be

everywhere
that earth-laden shadows
bride and bridegroom
keep
their swaddled flocks.

1981

Ode

I.

Interior of stone is stone   of water, water   in stone the lichen skein
in water, weft   Stone interiors are emptiness spaced wide
all that be empty is all wavering full   Interior of wood from want, joined
of water, woven threads of void   Dark over dark, dark
Arm-wings folded round the heart pulse within the heavy laden blackness
of the long clicking night.

II.

Flute flow
follows
bluing, to chee
p̈ watery
Bronyx
cackle.
Thrush any
thrushway
feathers its nesting heart in
egg brown speckle
hatched from onyx night when
round down dawn sliver
silvers
rivers
o

III.

Toe tries
to twig
and then when
double double beat
it
flyz hup

One red reed reach
just one red
leaf just one
red
poep
rd
ha

IV.

Be
needle's gold outpointing light thru fan-thin lines in leaves
in which reverberates the note hard hit: irradiated
love

whose every single
cell sounds all
as white, as light
the color chord entire;

each never-rounded
arcing shell
binds birth to ocean hearts
as much as burst with dark.

V.

Blue breath warbles watery fours
gold breath threes on earth
red spot tuneful voice from high
moist and dry
cold and hot

pulls the massy birth along
sequacious of the lyre's
leaf/leaf.

VI.

Swung over by green star-luminous bugs
under hairy leaf   under swollen leaf
half-hollow spots of living light
mistaking earth for heaven
so vast the ancient sounding
spheres so loose
the braiding flimsy
shimmer
everlasting you
over and under under.

Black hold among holes   hope among holes   black
stones green flashy bugs woof
steady in the air that threaded planet plurals;

space, size,
affirm another orb or two;
hums up inside the wires in the neck
a warp dark tree.

Muck heads in the mudrich mulch under
Night-fresh stars celestial sprouting over
specks of itchy antfast journeys
under earth's plain black bleak place and
white beaked over-eager
time:
those
underplayed and thrice displaced
designs,
random,

that untune the sky.

1981

Megaliths

Standing beyond the threshold of silence
they loom from the underbreath
stark so far and firm

On the gray flat horizon
the peer dancers
wet as mist in mist

These are the dancers
who beckon by waiting
the radical letter—

These the unwritten
vast before, vast after
bridging—

Where they are is space
where I am, blackfall.

Place, place
I cannot do no longer—

But they are statues of my body speaking:
the way of the poem
is the way
of this
border
the rising—
a dark, treacherous
water—

altocumulus
of a chaotic sky
coming to the end
of which
if it
is not all
path
it is no path

All the horizon

is the abyss:

floodfill, maps clog
clayey with matter; mud
swaddles the engorged feet:

a dull flame
flats, tight, lowered to hiss,
so that the merest

moves mark to mark and makes a crossing
into boundless dance.

breath, blows its own out
by very empty dark.

i.m. M.K.
1980, May

32

Two Gypsies

Two gypsies camped across the woods,
  I heard their sharp guitars.
I wanted them to read my hand
  and tell my stars.

I went down the darkened path
  the leaves I brushed withdrew.
The trees flew up and stood so tall
  they masked the moon from view.

They told me a man had come to them
  from far beyond the hill;
they said our fortunes were the same
  but told no ill.

And more I asked and more I stayed
  their answers were so bold.
The fire danced a wild wild way
  that forbade cold.

And back along the darkened track
  the dew that once so light
shone from the bracken on the path
  had thickened with the night.

The time grew pale, my pace grew slow.
  The chill wind before morn
was vacant of all fiery glow.
  I felt two times forlorn.

And emptied of what I had found
  was emptied of my self.
I saw a shadow cross my own.
  I turned and wept.

There was a man beside me there.
   His hair was dark with sweat.
His face was white as mine, and fair.
   His eyes were jet.

"I ran to catch you here," he cried.
   "You were too fast," he said.
"Come and stay here by my side."
   He took my hand.

And turned with me along my path
   nor would I dry my tears,
so let them fall as if another
   dew upon the leaves.

And where he has the rage to go
   I can prevent it not,
with my one trial of stepping fro
   looped back into a knot.

The ribboning path that led beyond
   has tightened this befall,
has bound my eyes to not look out,
   has me in thrall.

And so the man beside me there
   on my right side and my left.
He said my fate was in his care.
   I stood bereft.

1962/1983

Moth: *"Ode to Psyche"*

— 1 —

Percussive throws of the moth-
gambler moth-die
moth-face soft face
hurtling
from one edge of the pegged down screen to the other.
Twang of wire, wing
rag(e)s bug "burning" with desire for some bright torch
: dark clustered tree-eyes beyond
and moonless scattered fanes of night
thin stars without a name beyond unreachable light
THROWS
the ovoid winged egg at the emplacement
one dry page casement.

— 2 —

Across the level feather-mottled body
rock laden visitors of skin
blackened with feeling
clitoral police,
flat ope on the barrier.
Blank the room you thrill to enter
no flourishes, outrigger, no oracle, no voice.

Mealy-winged moth desires flat
slapping whn desires unveiled
moth eyes of high obsession random
moth splay brown mark under eye,
pale-mouthed prophet
pounds the raging promise half articulated
into the fabled space of unconstricted possession
marked by pinpoints, orange "inhuman" sight
that squint into the proper book of light.

3

Macerated by the acrid air
One blank ghost haunts the window
one gaping sob one boy strangling
his mother grasping round her warm neck
he grabs to love in rage.
Two wings and strike like a snake
the moise noise wehing wehing.

What imago of fast movement
would long for these embittered aspects?
Fulgurous fans, beat out, away, away
beat wrung from this insipid image's
nay-said repeated drum
whose garbled sobs can just in "dream-weep" come.

4

Ah but the liminal sickness, t   hwup the blank moth
heaves again its pallid self
against the divisor, lightning splits the center
brain: two halves one ghosti
against the fleshy doorway;
The lungs wing out ple ple hitting
constrictions of breath.

So the winged worm throws, thrills to
the fastness, habitual the stubborn moth
plastered against some unread, light-filled tome,
it makes delicious moan.

5

Knife thread
cloth of night and you once spun inside it
feeling the promise of, the void of trains

Writing in the station notebook all the codes
broken, a vision
white and brown moth feathering against
the hard square of "its" desire.
Resisting normal linkages
barnacled thoughts of the psyche
forsaken, her moth-mouth working
pursing pursuing
so much hitting
stolen time has baffled.

She strings herself through fond believing lyre,
she stuns herself against the form of the window—
the screen resounds in flat no tune no chord.
The utter wings dark scorch
yet still demand, compel, another's bright(er) torch.

—6—

Wrapped forever. Dim blankets turgid pinions.
And bitter, hitting words onto the sketch pad
cool rooted resistance shredded
Pen-sylvia station sheets banded together
so no one would steal, no one would
steal a-way into a pouch, she tucked the won ones
into oracles.

Wrath of the layered silence to avenge.
Bundled a human packet
exists to this day where Broad
crosses Columbia trussed
a message band(i)ed bonded in leaves of rags and ropes
for she alone Alone
inedible rage,
her thready fascicle.

OR piled both word and page
the brown winged cast of

harvested leaves
at the violent barrier;
threw down her spotted self
by blunt flight gamble-led
the snake eye double die did stop the game dead.

—7—

The one who killed a psyche-elf, the openness too heavy
the one who walked up to the silent tower daily:
it must begin now, but never does;
how to protect them from their desire to leap
into the rigid square of light
because there is at once too much and much
too little.

The fullness that rises hungers for fullness
YET tamp(er)ed down,
heel hard on a pupa, the silent mingled organs,
no voice, no lute, no pipe, no lucent fans,
no more the essential elements' distinction
delicate within a solemn perfect insect
able to spin a being from itself.

The eye is out forever, it will never be united.
Mark where the space was; rebus its dread hole.

The difference between dead and living?
One fur-thready filament, from the silk gland
of a rejected and panicked giving
whose central rage goes into living.

—8—

Like a block of stone carried forever, like mutilation
death and fear are constantly present,

not in the portal,
not in the insect
but somewhere, some place some basalt place
the unutterable
bond between them, endless battering.
Gravel sobs quickly stifled
what shadowy thought can win these outcries back
from burial.

Sinuosities, wings rising from a single seed
in the stone
the pupa sullen, snuggles, thick with time
nay-said   nascent   any birth?

The hatchling in the vetchling
the changes   the furrows
dazed with dismal prophesies
so far retired
from happy pieties.

—9—

The grub is in dirt.
Never at peace with the immeasurable moistness
of hope,
did branch its thoughts beyond one swirled
single slug,
eye-dawn rising over eye dark midnight.

Not breaking, hardly breathing, apnea
of the worm
in the dewy carbon of the ground
wakens itself as from a bubbling pool
of silent drowning.
The acrid space it seized
rich with lichens against which it takes its ease.

It is the moss-lain flesh blue rider
that struggles gleefully and wide
through the book leaf matted down
through the dumped seasons
puply choirs of musclefarting
eating hot up.

The wild worms swirl
the small grubs curl
under

writing lines of eager slime
black and rotten warmth, cell-meaty mass
rooted in the muddy and blank
tunnels the multitudinous tuneless numbers,
bareness blaring unarranged.

1983–84

Oil

bei Dickinson

The oil that rises every month
as oracle of moon
slides sleekly from the strata wells—
a panther in the bush—

or where there was the hush that comes
just when the power moves
beyond the stands where we are happy,
rooted as we are—

when solid Silence drops away
and from a hole beyond
the darkest Gush
will geyser up
as brilliant as the sun.

Just the universe again
that voices from the Void—
Abyss is not an absence
though presence be destroyed.

Var. for l. 13 and last stanza

as brilliant as the sun—

and cover sun, though sun is bright,
so force is faced obscure—
a knowing darkly in the Rush
that light can not answer.

1978

Attar

There's a Nerve along the Jaw
   That Dentists call Attar.
They operate within these Threads'
   Essential Jugular.

Why They held me in the Chair
   How found that subtle, bloody Hair,
Who "They" were, why They appeared
   I could not Face to tell.

"What is the Nerve You Like to Cut?"
   "We call it Attar."
And inched with Tools into my Spot
   The Root Canal to strike.

Articulate with Diagnoses
   They Probed along the gum,
Mapped each particular to Clamp
   The Jets before they come.

Contesting Doctors—unseemly.
   Shriek? Weep? Query? Rebut?
Why did I ask but what They called it?
   Not *"Why do You Cut?"*

1984

Blues

Yellow mustard spikes,
marshy water lily bright.
I got a little golden lock where I
threw away the key,
a combination lock
where the numbers go 1-2-3.

Wanted to turn my life's work
inside out
Yeah she said   she wanted to turn
her work into something else,
said she wanted to talk about
spitting into a drought.

I got a ballad and a blues
like a big hand-lettered sign.
It's a down turn note
in a song that's on my mind.
Confiscating that tune
three voices on the back of my mind.

There's a trouble-trouble child
and a middle-size long-time man.
Lock away from the child,
turn away from that long time man.
Look out of my window and I
twist my heart for wrath.

Got the blue note in my ear
But I can't get it out of my mouth.

1983

Sister Rachel's Spirit Tree

I'm giving gifts from the giving tree
A ou na na   Ah u na nee
Great flower of glee in the heart I find
Your hands and mine will both be filled.

A cake of love I give to you
So eat it down with loving bites
Slivers of nutmeg sprinkeled on it
I le vou nee.

A little pudding love
I give Vou Nee,
One drippy drop in the bottom of the cup
A drop of sweetest silver wine.

A root of cress and growing cressy
I bind in a sheaf and a leaf beside
from the willow-hung waters
flowing by my side.

Feed me crumbs just like a bird
and I will weep just like a bird
and I will sleep just like a bird
cheeping pee shee on the sound of gifty.

Then sweep it clean
I will, my mother

Sweep clean as the tree
I will, my love

O sweep the drone the shining
company of sorrow

So we can walk over meadows clean.

1981

44

Afterimage

He has entered the space between
   himself

and his dying

in that breath thru which
   homeless

the pearly waters rose to make mud.

No plan. It is land
   unnamed.

The deep oily

thoroughfare, no more primitive
   element, no

going backwards, no leaping

backwards, away
   from finding blackness.

                    .

Between darkness and light

before the white thread can be told

from the black before it is

palpable, how to tell

both how

can the black road be

white, the dark field mirror tolled

half-blank, how to toil and not

see Self?

.

Dark field, white mirror half-blank there
is a vanishing point.

Your eyes wide and inward,
your eyes watch your eyes still
watch yourself
cast in and cast out.

There is a vanishing
bottom of a fathomed place.

.

Soft
at the hillside crumbles   the brown moist
edge

inward;
here pools naked water   a scum green rises
within.

.

Because
it was not situated
and could not rise nor fall relative to
anything

he walks,
going on quietly

into something

enraged with annoyance
as with banality and also
peace. And time.

.

Legacy?

Sometimes every one else seems

perfectly unworthy:

bonfire crisps; flash floods; glass costs.

These the obstacles.

People are inhuman as disease.

Is everything for the last time?

What use was it ever?

.

And earth.
Its powers.

It must not have a name.

.

Walks holding
a silver thread into
a water maze

flooded with

everything
tries to see to seize

changes he
ebbs and flows
around his silver body.

.

Terse riddings.
Riddled turnings.
What little shells in baskets over
and over the shells
from nameless emptied creatures!

The shadow round the bone
patiently
complies.

Why indeed should I not be

one

of them?

.

The little thems.
Forgive yourself.

.

Watch, watcher into the night a
new, cool rustling   darkness without
shadow   rictus   total.

These things   probably true.

.

This crossing a river by walking
under a river.

Black hole in a universe of seeds.

.

Flat black stones smoothed in the whorl
wind of water, so.

Sometimes I want to avenge bread.

.

No doors.
Do not ask for any.

.

Swum into the cool of the lake (innocently)
found the icy updraft
feed and pull
hidden body tangles swimming body.

.

The hand cups.
It is not enough.
The hands cup.

Earth spring
swings sweet in the deepened hillock.

The drinker has fluttered the surface
reaching down:

must wait then
for the loose green floating

up from the earthen sides to still
to return to the hill

wait then for the pool's bud dark waters
to clarify.

.

Thirst that sudden and below
wells for other water.
The thirst was parched with life.
It bent to drink and quench.

.

1986

Selvedge

Leafflat self of cell and gem
whose living eye fills fathomless with pleasure—

on what tree? and by what beak?
and ho what noted e of speech?

Silly many my likenesses; all is
leaves, birds, all birds is greens

and sing
the pretty boobies in the trees:

below, above, below, above;
in sum there is no "where."

: :

Linked listings un-
to, say,
mine unto thine,
unripe berry

red circle
bordering greeny sphere

await itself inside itself

ripens   a rustling   my-

self ragged half-pecked cells that hang
together;   porous   flickering
"while"
plural seed-filled thought.

: :

Samara

samaras

green   sleeves

make a moon
round rainy trees.

If more seeds fall
will I learn the nature of rain?

Gather the borders snug,
pupal,
eat the teachers,

all under the bosky grids of time and place
and under wreathe my boughs.

1980

II. Drafts

Writing

.Smudge, ballpoint, iridesces
behind the.

Oily shadow grains an entry
scrap.

Night
underpainting
confident. An a.
Black lines
dot nylon rope about,
tie scout knots.

What paths inside
other
territory of utterance
hear me

smudge and hear me

whiteness

.Plum grainy
veins, unfathomable
noises, moues and wrinkle
winkle

Plumb line, pul-
sing, eye to eye, drinks
dusks of light.

One year after, like a punctuation; one month together, and these
times had meaning, particular meaning, were also an arbitrary path
cut through possibly a mistaken hole in the floor, they thought the ra-
diator was smaller, and there it is, an unfilled circle ninety years old.

full moon, and hardness   My mother I will, she said.

.A wri-
ting marks the
patch of void
foggy reflecting
mist catches wet carlight

that everything tests
condenses
refracted silence
The cold rush up
the dark dark trees
Somnulent spots of travel

film
fine tip flairs
baby wipes
khaki thread
nipples

Letters are canal-
ized as white foams
zagging, a fissure on the
sheet,

tangle of branches unorganized without the leaves
cock-eyed underbelly of
plenitude of

mark. *outtakes, can imagine conversations?*
conversions?
Long passages of satisfaction swallowed up
in darkness.

SO MANY DISTANCES INTO INVENTION
.sing way–
ward black   A TREK. ACROSS SLUGGISH
against grey brown against END-WINTER GRASSES, BARK SCRAP
black gave small   TWIG BLOWN, LIMB DOWN A ROT
twig   AND FEATHER-WHITE WOOD
s un stinting   ALL SCRABBLE AND GROUND

Without silver
remarks without glistening   UNITCHED VERY ITCH
tone the little feeling touch   (imbeddings, angles)
light as it is
what is that   BUT SUCH A BIG AREA, SO MA,
the.
             LEAVES
             AND THEY BLOW
             THEY BLOW
             THEY BLOW.

.Voracious swelling ocean all
smallest possible words of all

To a
time thickened initial
the tee

                        have so many little tasks

which oscillation
speeding, seems to fix.

                        picking this and tending that
                        my back hurts

Both a cut for "beginning," a
historical
sequence the poem invites
mastectomies
of dice

and a wrapping, random,
buntings of stories
carried, carried dearly
to the other side of weeping
(could never credit the whole story)
precious bundle.

*handwriting, written
story-wise on the canvas
close in
any square inch of standing here,
intensity overlayering boredom.*

.Fructifying inundation of
alien corn
offers groundswell.
Grey crocii pearly
sprout, snowlogged, slimy,
dying consensual.
The plot was so big it
encompassed all

Pink swans
"Utopian" living in the deep

abyss!

statements. Thick black
cover lined pages.
Thus it is

maybe political cynicism with odd
borders gerrymandered.

And, in the space between entropy
and arousal,

Philomel,

or, longing for liquid
song.

.word. Blue

(pants, trousers, cover-
alls) Blue, all
tempered drop
into
the morning bizniz sweet
whistles, their hustle low
the-y fl-y one (tows) three.
Stroke in the air, wobble
a tune, wow.
Two red tickets set at an angle—

"There is Mr. Ashley, narrating
his 'songs' or 'stories' in a
gentle, sing-song chant—what
he terms 'vocal inflections
that you might call singing.' "

Imbedding some   extruding some   the interplay between selection,
imbedding, and loss. Some few words, chosen, and why; but are also
chosen from, once the day was awash in pinpricks, a pull in the back
muscle, overlay and no experience. No experience because all. Say.
Saw. **Operations. Addictions. And no** shadow and it was dark within
this icy **one knows** brightness all disappearing all intense
writing **what;** does it save it? "diaristic" in impulse, but
unbargained, imponderable. Over written. Written then over written,
over ridden, the selection is one thing, this (the globule, clot) another.
Different plans and different pictures.

Most poetry something—	uneven picture patterns, irregular blocks, a rebus trued, held in a rose-pink border.
imagery, structure.	

Dreaming I'm crying
it's she's crying.

Making her and watching her

.All like little novels?   *make herself*
Novels are nothing like this.
           The synchronicity of seeing that when
          this—
Too many subplots   *it goes along—*
bleating   *I can't keep it in mind if I*
chaotic lambs   *don't connect*
on the territory
of utterance   *repress, it*
unfurling,
as well, deep night   *(as it)*
reinvents ab-
straction, blueness,   *goes along.*
as, say, gay
day does (sometimes)   sometimes visually
syntax.   stated "imperfection"
            material "run-
out" added a piece of red
           "accidentally" reversed two
patches, inserted an "un-
           matching" background slash.

.Snaggles, spiggles, stalks
peck out snow.
Fresh, purple, haiku,
heuristic.

little wails cringing at the sight of green. the hand
that takes the pacifier out the mouth cannot (wail)
yet put it in. me puts it in, o me.

mouth moth(er)

.Face face face face-y
without particularity
mouth, dots, la la La la LA
have to learn that flat is flat   props. shitskies.
In baby in-   phone. no. ba-ba.
undation of contexts.   what; was wet.
                                         next door.
                                         Odd time of
                                         year to be moving.
Impossible maybe to write
the techne of dailiness the hand reaching onto the shelf the
dust
collected in a particular corner   the objects also a little
dusty with the spring light through the back door   objects
directly in the sunlight   the coupon torn or cut, saved
as a lacy proof of thriftiness   the unmendable cracks this,
attempt at exactness, is readable the intersecting rhythms of
muscles small muscles when cutting when sorting how
to assimilate   how to discuss   to represent
the pulses of pleasure and heartlessness   to ascertain
fairly the moon small cadences
dotty lights
rust rough ride shod cracks
the surface
winnow the pillars
what kind of a deal
anyway
all this has been "the"
just where I thought I began
beyond.

.Winking mer
ry
mi mer rill
lea
toy houses each with
toy family and the gigantic
swollen viviparous rivers
flooding silences that never
get drained.

.Letters: a readable staining
inked jelly floats loosely
lacking pectin.
Paper: thick rags, even, sometimes
flowers   leaf bits.

A rose weathers out of the page
o death
a strawberry out, greedily, of jam
a finger, a bud who
curls there, comma,
period, sky-reading
marks
creating marks   for "others" (ellipses) . . .

Borderline takes many forms

"not erasing the original signatures of the women"

"keep the noises as close to the body as possible"

.Stark. Melt. Still.
Terribly cold it wails   blurs
                                   unimpeachable travel
translucent mucus   ambush of cloud
Am I limpid?
Sing-song
for the sake of conversation
wet baby, dry baby.
Poetry
too much, too many.
White stone or green water,
some "coral," rareness, an occasional "amber."

People worry the ends of novels,
marry. Sonnets like novels.
Still lives encode bounty.
Still,
smudging these discourse cross-
hatches terminii

the end (ends up) every
where.

birds   .cumulus color of red sandstone, coal shale   resume
they   and close tabulated bunching   resume
re they   unfirm unpleasant undulent   re who
tcho   unconscious   tcho

pattern up   crests, its opposite   pitter pity
hole in the   touching hard and fast   they poke a
house   disperse   little nest
                  thick places
                  bound to violent narratives.

.Isolate animal
squeaks; a few weeks
later, impossible even to
remember

threw balled up newspapers for
flare on the fire

                          The distinction between city
                          and contado cannot be defined
                          by city walls.
a mewling into maybe milky dark.

mirror of dream milk smile mirror of actual noticing

.Undesired acts. Could code.
or the novel?

A meadow grey with sink holed   I have removed the finance
snow, melt drops foot-
prints through a whitish   charge of $2.11 and you
song
(add patched out   may look for this adjust-
brown). Acts of attention?
what an angle you make   ment on your next, that
on acts of inattention.
                                  is, your May, statement.
Curlicues meet curricula;
much roaring on all sides.
It's judgment.
Otherness sidles over to around
otherness
outcrops

more or less.

Writing (along the lines of research, of work   into and along
the lines of somethings together
as long as it, as they interest each other, trace into and
mark each other)   summarizes and accomplishes intermittent
yearning and proposals
that define the intersecting of strongly acknowledged yet
loosely defined materials with an "I" who is the hidden
subject and object of each of these verbs.

.A red squall-pulse glaums on
Nip eats (has eaten)
the tippy top the creaminess
forever. Could eat almost forever
depends   formula—Similac
on what convention
of satiety.

on feeling dopey

So how
does one ever
know? How
feed the fullness?

How to be that which is unspoken   how to speak that which is
"repressed"   elusive anyway   tangential   different
impending space   different enough   how to write that which
is / is

unwritten.

.Some words much
syntax or
allusions thereto
some invention, but
if *the laws*
of language are
socio-
logical laws then poetry
is provisionally
complicit resistance.

The poet's wife, old woman,
hunched in the kitchen drying
dishes, the whole
interview. Such things
happening on the side.
What is realism
made of?

The bitterness of already
unspoken bitterness?

your soul—
out!
—among the little

spaces
before entropy
(foreground, bulbous foyer)

becomes arousal
sparrows?

Narrative as betrayal?
keep going

Verification (Docu-
mentation): What
types to verify
my evidence?
Statistics?
Expert testimony—
quoted, paraphrased,
or summarized?
Personal experience
or eyewitness accounts?
Opinion polls
or surveys?

Language as betrayal?

betrayal of "what?"

keep going

.Walls
of words make turns   themselves
too prissy otherwise   red scarf
drops staining   a gossamer
reads   reds
through the book each page
an escarpment   tired
rems the book   red   flicker
of movement cardinal
o eyes go forward forward
little eyes on the plate, saint
carries her staring obvious odd place
trail of whispy
red in a white
space   the open square
between   letters   a piazza
of unlikeness.

.One anorectic,
or undigestible,
wedges into exits invented
unique. Locked in
zone
combat trinkets a few tiny
tears (of
amazement)
(of blocked)

just a sketch for the novel;
the plot is
"finally grieving."

.Live in meditation? dopey
Live in words?

whose?

Winter empty spikey weedy
and too tall.

I had mourned my mother
before it
happened she said

nothing touched   off nothing
potato salad   always the same word
ruined
no recovery no change.

This is a day   this wailing cold and no
"work" done   the blankness of receipt
no "papers" marked   a kind
of revulsion to every

thing no

"poem"

Marginalia without a center? No beginning, No. No
.One word one   *ending? No, because form*
"word" kkhkkhgggh   *at all times is instilled. O noble*
Koré la la   *that ongo-*
threaded into the dyad *ingness that entrance into speaking*
both ends beading, gleaming
gargle. Conventionally, "goo gah."   encapsulated
                                                      eyes burning
Big finger to the little sleeping mouth
                              It was all cracking
makes sure,

the even silence breathing.

Narrative: the oedipal plot? ends by revealing the hidden
father. Pre-oedipal plot? the mother, hidden. Split subject:
"a living contradiction." A text to speak now, writing,
writing the sung-half song.

.Jonquils, ruffled perianth,
rains beat them down,
a few
more
bulbs split
their green
arrowheads. Not a question of
making images. Making
what?

Climax? Silence? Poignant?
Points? The Memorable?
Fleshy thick the -y suffix
added means pleasure or cuteness
Silly Banilly

the word passes phatic or elegant
passes bonded passes through
grammar to get past syntax's single borders
to funny half-seens, stumbles;
all routes, all specks, all
snarled in matted eager acts.

.Is there new plot?   "this is not it"
chickens is there?   "it is not yet"
                          "now and nowhere"
"another"   now/here know now
poem roseate   no where
ones   near?

.A self that had already been formed
prior prior prior

opening these wounds

may
balkbalk balk
vast moody plunge

imbibed the emotional need
from notes. The oldest stratum
extruded disfunctionally.

Yearning for the syntax of time,
the "coral clasp" wobbling nicely,
some fancy meter

message like a taxi

Rereading this ha ha

(phone ringing)

.The torso fleurie *wanting to have her book virtually nameless*
flying vagini under full sail
twirl out a leaf print *what is the most transparent name?*
the point, sweet business,
treads water *is everything, or enough — so that*

        we are where

charging janus penis janus
thick right at the cusp

        we are.

slowly cover the space
bright disc harken

      what were the women like?
down down down *Evidence he wrote in The Vita Nuova: They*
by the orbiting ocean. *travelled together*
and commented incessantly on Dante's
red blotches

his leaning weakly against a wall
for love.

.Purple crocus cluster, saffron letters at the core
skid that shimmies the back wheels

(cho)coherence. incho(col)ate
debate. Best explanation
I've found
of overeating.

Dark blood and a little grinding

spur, a vector, and a little
more of something.

There is otherness coming from
otherness.

White telescope inside
slides
a packet of batting
me part is fulled with paper.

Invisible staining
a bubble one two three four arcs
        flake of clotting or something

It's all part of being
part of me
beet red drops at the bottom
of pee

of me making this
this end and of

just happening.

period.

But in writing?

Just one event among flux,
the many yet so
foregrounded
as fourth, maybe the sixth
tampax in writing?

1984–85

writing on "Writing"
   notes made between 15 March and 4 April 1985

Writing from the center of, the centers of, otherness.
Making otherness central.
Taking myself as central, yet in all my otherness. Trying to write Otherness when it is sometimes felt, or stated repeatedly, that otherness is the opposite of writing, although it may inspire writing.

Understanding formal marginality. Marginalization.
Setting the poem so there is a bringing of marginalization into writing.
"No center" of a section alternates with small contained sections.
Sections contained by other sections, over writing, writing over, or simultaneous with. So that one section does not have hegemony. So the reader does not know which to read first, or how to inter-read.
(And one procedure, adjudicated for one particular section, will not carry over or be applicable to another section. So that one does not learn mechanically; the reader is at large, as the poet is. We are strained companions.)

Part of the debate, or a contribution to the debate, between literature and writing. (Silliman said poetry and writing, I think)

Putting that debate right in the piece by making several sayings or statements be in the same page-space. Making poetry and writing be in the same page-space. Making alternative poetries be in the same page-space.

As to subject: a first or really second month of a baby who comes as otherness, as difference, which cannot necessarily be understood easily, but demands to, needs to be felt, understood.

          : a menstrual cycle, the very core of female difference (they say. Sometimes we say) over centuries of our culture. Getting that into writing.

          : spring coming: certain flowers certain anger and resistances. Cool weather, never as warm as one would like.

      : creating marks: pen, smudge, letters, things that make marks or take impressions (Baby wipes). Handwriting (inc. in text). Repression in mind. Writing to remember. Drawing distinctions. Things on the side, things in the center, blurring distinctions.

      : how/why/what to write: realism, recording, selection. Allusions to cross genre, or messing up.   (quilts)   Genres that create themselves as imperfect. To write into silence. *The.* And the *t.* Narrative and experience. "Narrative" and "experience." Poetry too pretty; creating "beauty"? Creating chora.   Beginning–middle–end, ha.

And as to image flash, there is inscription, writings of all sorts to be read and gleaned. Usually black and white. Intermittently, there is an almost unfollowable flash of (flesh of) red or a related color. Red is the trace or signal of otherness. Signalling like that (red flag) is probably one of the more traditional aspects of this poem. Of this writing.

Draft #1: It

N.

   N.

      ==

and something spinning in the bushes   The past

                        dismembered   sweetest
          dizzy chunk of song
                        one possible: there is a
in another   strange erosion and
dready fast flash   all the sugar is reconstituted:
                              sunlight
silver backed   as 'stem'; sugar as dirt.
light this
governed being: it?   that?

plunges into every object
a word and then some   chuck and
pwhee wee
half
tones
have tunes's
heft.

      ==

One day lose him her
One day lose them

then it melts and dusts tomorrow too.
Me long   gone dissolutions   of
chucnk and humming a-
ddress it.
             have seen faces of limestone, stone cold piled
             unmortered, wandering, dividing the ranges; it
             lettered on green up hillside's social lining.
             divisions and elaborations of property, land-
             scape striated with historical sentence.
             have seen sheep, knolls, pebble turds in piles.
             A mark, a tuft, a makr   a/ a\
makes meaning it's
framed marks that make
meaning is, isn't
it?   Black

coding inside   A
white fold open   eye
open   a little
slip

        = =

To what purpose reveal details of fleshy registers one
CAN have, blah blah   their charm? It's not
irony (really); it's awe.
They are what we are, we are
that,
that's it; it's only what we are,   we write our bodies
all and only what   begin space
(maybe)   by talking
the tizzy dizzy spin   at the window the
stars; a meaning's point   laid lines   weather

perfect,   the turnings talk
                                  in it;
                                      two shadows blown

is one way of hinting it.

          = =

It is not surprising that   where in the placement of
                                saffron this is simple 'you'
It is not surprising,   are listening 'I' am alert
that.   enough 'she' is learning how to
                                talk 'we' are reconstituted.
It
is not surprising That.   This is the spoilage of
                                presence   a condensation of
It's the little stuff that slips the wink   rot ick or
slides past phatic   split tingle
under all those sheets   "what
dog is woofing"   what shuttle
brights what warp?   WATER damage it really needs
                                replacement

Can I heed   you, it?   This line, scrawl of a bird line
                             tide line

          = =

                             I feel the
The strange light scuds
jewels   to say
anything (it) must be   half-eaten apple

mistrusted.
                             wedged under me in the car.
It must be loved like milk.

          = =

(parole prevailing against long)

It, is so
long.

== ==

To reinvent "attention" is narrow tho tempting.
Doesn't get the folding.   I
is it
                        The
                                generative
nor jargons in antiphon   mist
I always thought "antiphon" was the most

fat shadow.   beautiful word.   slight show.

                        A white house seems
                        to be a further
                        coagulation of mist
Lucite see-thru overlay, mark upon mark
glistening thru those microtimes of day. Stein in short was

No postcard poetry, a this a that like
a boat like a dog and not just any dog but   eliding
an over-eager retriever on waves   over
maybe like chickens bobbing.   the over.

== ==

CANO, can o,   yes   no
conno-
tations of impurities fill the fold.
Why that, or why
"sea blazed gold"
why
re-up anyway, to artifack

art pac, o me
o my.

== ==

Nostalgia for a touch
resistant how
the language forms of sweetened
clouds   for fat and white   I love
you   Little whirlwinds of paper caught in the
clouds   cross-currents of systems (skyscraper wind
as clouds   tunnels, roads cut, built, then lined with
shadows creased in heaps and brights   delicate
                                     garbage, a land-
not literally thighs.   lessness even as we squat here so
                      on the land we are) the

            lyric?

== ==

putt (pitting) the tiny word
litt
it
on stage in a "theatrical" space
a
space white and open a flat
spot a lite on
it   something
alight like wings.

Well now what's
to speak what is
to speak when that
Object (pronoun)
squeaks its little song its bright white
dear dead dark.

I hear, I do. YO! hear it
hear "it"? hand it into the wings.

dat dat dat
didn't want any beauty
tender
but

theater of the

       page   cream   space   peaks

    = =

    where in the space of particularity one passes
    beyond ego; where in the placement of saffron
MA ME I AM A WAKE a   and black tuft of heide, no
hoy ma milky-moo   hurt to the heath, not hold
bright boo.   the heart is empty being so
    full of a calmness marking minute practice.

    = =

Let silence
    in the form of words'
            in.   IT.

    = =

Some ART today:
a
mimetic use of mottled crepuscular marble to make a
pop ice cream
cone of,
vidi (!),
I saw—impossible
NOT to argue in light of it.

I'll make a representation
to you about it
later. After I end my song.

Shame is ordinary. Shamelessness
just a bit less. The real
interest is
limpidity,
power, the necessary

no and yes.   I wouldn't want to spread
Nos and Yesses incessant.   myself too pointedly.

        = =

There's no way to read it?
One point is to achieve a social momentum of switched
referrents and (merry coral   white clover
ding ding ding) commentary in which what   he (you)
says or does must be read differently from what she
does or says whether he, you does it to her or them to
it (of whom?) she to it feels different (nights of Holly-
wood fascism) in an unsettling but not articulate way.
power power imbedded in, in its   (days of military realism)
place on the pronoun grid, cells squeak in protest "it's
just language" "we're just nature"

        = =

TORN FROM (A PAGE)

a kind of orange it happens
a kind of orange
IT HAPPENS
rose rinse, vertical green.
Away anyway has shadow
"a typical Rachel shadow"

blue starts limb long and torso struggles
its window when all around there's not a single
wall, NO blockages
hardly stopped at all except by the pleasures
of color are you getting the picture
it hpps BLUEW one from the sequences of looming
comes   longing

                = =

There's *no;* read *it.* Down
under where broach is, a
nuzzle a quick fat. It is the
"it" characteristic of everything.   Yes, read it!

        A narrative, a story, a plot, every word "a plot
        against the reader"; coagulations of it, rays
        pleased to be doing what they're doing not cynical yet

        and plenty spaces

                = =

The struggle from whiteness
into whiteness
via black wit-

ness

I

ching.

        = =

Overlope loop. Laugh language laugh.
Sandstone reach overload wrack
parabolic pools, warm line harken
shells   I
want to be *in* it, but it is not for
in it   it

is it.

Little girls little legs jump the wine dark line.

== =

No "books"   no ministers   no tow art

"no sandpoems"   build of it, not on it

it is sacred what you can do with it

the general aura of quest just as a baseline.

This silence awash with

bodies   flowered   aglow astripe to be

folded over signals.

Words' ribbon-wing hover, hovers, hovering.

Silence, silence, silence

was, this was, the implicit subject was

never foolhardy.

== =

Silences are the reaches of discourse

(rich incipit's big initials)

There is a yes and a no walled welled up

Sorrow? weeping yes and weeping no

it   is the definition of speaking;

gladness too is it, its weeping.

Silence is not the only subversion; it is.

The letters rise into a consuming which makes more

black fire flaming on white fire.

Fire fear (fears) fire. Scared is sacred.

Black arrow shot in blacker sleep

green word fold in greeny pock of folk

Speak, quiver, before your waves grow destitute

Dark feather dropped in foam of darker, antecedent sea.

          = =

May 1986–January 1987

Draft #2: She

The white one turns red they say
then peach to white   grass rich the edge-fold
space

slices of porcupine deep undergound
and et that red-grained fat.

"I be good girl with my magic
markers."

(marks hands up red
makes henna dark touch)

Taboo thy ruses, moues and roses, shh.
Terracotta, ochre smear of Provence
shadowy stains
       stairs ·

Ask for danger, say

"I want that danger."

^ ^
 ·

Who has

how images rise
            rinse and erase how

can the rose
speak and how much

can you in fact stand that lobotomized
memory you have been washed up
into
do you

NO?

Dear (name),
        I (morder)
                for departure's sake
further reaches.

The thin voice of the thin space.
Red red the rushes rise
down down by the salt tide veil, that
Love depicted as against itself:
small happy (guillotined) family unit
petal lashed to petal.

^ ^
 .

Families set like junket IN milky rooms'
schematic valleys—
V-shape of the young runnel;
rennet sweet-white jellies
over cascades of russet granite.

^ ^
 .

Lightly risen, of a plastic
pink too close, too
bare,
tho luminous Food one could imagine there
the Moone
when next I spy
retracts: a dime-size toy-tied dish my moony

quest too dumb to ask a better question.
                              bitter

Still such catheter stuck there into my any fleck is
profligate.

^ ^
 .

jests
Of suggestive twists, of wax rib
joists

stuffed by a potential crime,
do you read her as
'Mother'? 'Woman'?

"Bandit
one-armed "Angel With A Lamp"?
"Badger

beam my way, beamy tinkling light; be me now
O Be Thou Me, sinuous one!

The piece, it's fleshy, picture perfect,
peachy . . . wax torqued up

fill
to fool this unrelinquished peephole.

Luminosities enormities of
key-shaped air in which she
flocks, twisted in brush,
sine curves verbatim.
A pubis allusive; the eye penises thru the keylock;
the eye is complicit and so is
HUNGER
NAUSEA
hurl
for I am afraid to hole it TOO MUCH
hurt

not speak of hold me.

"I am your danger."
"I am your anger, ranger."
"I am your angel, dudgeon."

^.^

Red orange with red veining
shading   raised
rib of same
color runs into large gold throat
suppressed heart, green.

Pale peach that by evening has a flush of pink

There is a pink rib goes
deep, up to the hilt,

rose heart, bound.
Between me? that?
heavy-eyed light gazing.

Daylilies open and drop
opal nenuphars of tears;

"I am your angle, stranger."

ˆ .ˆ

Each word a cryptogram
never too much:
in narrow, nah
in ride, rid
in courage, cor and rage

in flax phlox hemp feather, hook
garland   pull

a cryptic outline OF something
word shoal   staunched blood
food
stood at the edge of well-beloved veins

looking cock-eyed at all their deep,
at all their deep blue writing.

^ . ^

Shadow under-word
lopes thru stands of wet papyrus—
microclimates for this ploy
versus that: rain warms here; wind twists there;
one family eats well, another eats each other.

House of the soul is filled with little
things, clay vessels, slipped and glazed
all smallness green leaf offering;
sweaty flower; baby loaf;
small as half an envelope which wads up tight
the poem's patchouli.

In shires, shrines:
you're going to have something
about aging teeth, you're going to have left
something half-chewed
in front of that house,

food on the plate of the moon?
mets sur l'assiette de la lune?

That hard to write
"the mother"? to get that
empty for that full

mouth(e)

her(e)

sh(e) ?

^ . ^

A borer, a beetle, an eater,
who will evaluate hunger?

Bowel, bowl, daughter
whosoever siphons undigested words
requires a wide tube.

＾ ＾
.

Dabbles the blankie down
din
do throw foo foo
noo
dles the arror
of eros the error of arrows
each little spoil and spill
all during pieces fly apart.
Splatting crumb bits there and there.
Feed 'n' wipe. Woo woo petunia
pie.
Hard
to get the fail of it,
large small specks each naming
yellow surface
green bites
Red elbow kicks an orange tangerine.

The time inside, makes tracks, seems a small
room lurches into the foreground, anger, throwing, some
dash, power swirls up against MErock, pick it UP,
Mommy me NEED
it a push a touch a
putsch pull a flailing kick a spool
for her who is and makes thread
"I"
The she that makes her her
The she that makes me SHE

＾ ＾
.

Practicing ferocity on $\begin{smallmatrix}\text{your}\\\text{her}\end{smallmatrix}$ self

You become the mother   certainly a change.
            the monster   a chain.

        foaling
Is this failing the mother?
        finding

^ ^
 .

Top half poison   yellow light from above
ivy next half scritchings   blue light swells from earth
the garden red   bruising a frame

            Digging, I sit on a flower.

Counting the steps of bright shadow, the pure pause, paces
clusters of ripe tones making up loud and then whispy forces
across one singular place saying no to itself with meditative
privation, yet unfixed, so spun out of, *or* of, being or
seeing. Which is not, but as it starts, starts a little
rivulet sound and voice, another, it fuses, pivots, a sigh
and sign; desire's design, blue transparencies rich for
thirst   listen, to listen is to drink
how can there be
another   cry: whom; one of another, who?
who cries? who listens?
hear here the liquid light
swirl and merge with drinking calls.
A sigh, a moan from what is waiting. Sweet sweet
sweet teas(e)
Another cry, a honey voice

Another
one.

^ ^
 .

All told, a voluminous backdrop:
crevices of the night, 4:32 exactly
silver hush behind, curdling
a shaggy hurt bleat.
Eat that moon's sweet light.
Bird's blood is brown.
Her words, some said, they're just a
"bandaid on a mummy."

Wad reams of rems into mâché
my eyes chewing.
She screams unassimilable
first dreams.

Hold her unutterable

And press another quire of girl bound in, bond in, for pink.
Draw drafts of "milk" these words
are milk the point of this is
drink.

June 1986–January 1987

Notes on the text

I. *The "History of Poetry"*

"She cannot forget the history of poetry because it is not hers": from Joanne Feit Diehl, " 'Cartographies of Silence': Rich's *Common Language* and the Woman Poet," *Feminist Studies* 6, 3 (Fall 1980).

"The Poems of Sappho" contains transformed sentences and phrases based upon *The Poems of Sappho,* translated by Susy Q. Groden (Bobbs-Merrill Company, 1966) as follows:
   a chest for holding women's things, cf. p. 122; Edmonds 178
   a lyre, guitar and mandolin, cf. p. 122; Edmonds 178
   tender pillow, cf. p. 121; Edmonds 176
   two minds, cf. p. 30; Edmonds 52
   I want and yearn, cf. p. 15; Edmonds 23
   a dripping towel, cf. p. 67; Edmonds 131
   and over my eyes, cf. p. 98; Edmonds 141 A

Edmonds is *Lyra Graeca,* edited and translated by J.M. Edmonds (Harvard University Press, 1922). The phrase from Paul Valéry, "Le pain tendre, le lait plat" is from "Palme," *Poésies* (Gallimard, 1942). The pun on Homer is, apparently, Sappho's.

"Praxilla's Silliness." Work by Praxilla of Sicyon (c. 450 B.C.) is based on the translation by John Dillon in *The Penguin Book of Women Poets,* ed. Carol Cosman, Joan Keefe, and Kathleen Weaver (Penguin Books, 1980), and information in *Lyra Graeca,* vol. III. Her text was preserved only by the carping critic cited as epigraph. The end citation is worked from Praxilla; the mid-text citation is by H.D. from the manuscript "Autobiographical Notes, 1932—Greece," Beinecke Rare Book and Manuscript Library, Yale University.

"Madrigal," cf. Thomas Nashe, "Spring, the Sweet Spring."

"Rose." Ronsard, for the catch line "Mignonne, allons voir si la rose . . . " and Edmund Waller's "Go, lovely rose" for "common" and "fated."

"Crowbar." Dante is the source, quite modified, for some of the materials, including the vision of women in *La Vita Nuova* and a refabrication of both "Deh Peregrini . . . " and the sestina "Al poco giorno e al gran cerchio d'ombra." Bonibell from Spenser; Dés from Mallarmé. The Fontaine de Vaucluse is, besides being a notable geological formation, part of the Petrarch-Laura legend. A water-powered paper mill on the site fabricates paper imbedded with flowers.

"Killing Me." Thomas Wyatt, "They Flee from Me."

"Eclogue." The silly sheep are Spenser's.

"Ode." John Dryden, "Ode on St. Cecelia's Day."

"Megaliths." Read down each column, then across both.

"Two Gypsies." John Keats, "La Belle Dame Sans Merci."

"Moth: 'Ode to Psyche' " from John Keats, "ode to Psyche" with allusions to Sylvia Plath and Emily Dickinson.

"Oil" cf. the writing practice of Emily Dickinson

"Sister Rachel's Spirit Tree" contains "nonsense" syllables from Shaker song.

"Afterimage." D.H. Lawrence, "The Ship of Death"

"Selvedge," has "Greensleeves," traditional. The final line was a gift from George Oppen, based on my draft.

"Writing." William Carlos Williams, "January Morning"; Christopher Marlowe, "The Passionate Shepherd to his Love"; Julia Kristeva interview, cited in Teresa de Lauretis, *Alice Doesn't;* news article on composer Robert Ashley in *The New York Times;* Roland Barthes, *The Pleasure of the Text;* a comment by Robert Creeley; a statement by V.N. Volosinev, *Marxism and the Philosophy of Language.*

"Draft #1: It." "Torn from (a page)" is the title of a painting by David Hannah; the section contains allusions to other of his paintings. The quip about "Rachel" from a letter by Kathleen Fraser. There is an allusion to a statement by Paul Celan.

"Draft #2: She." The artwork alluded to in the fifth section is Marcel Duchamp's *Etant Donnés,* an installation at the Philadelphia Museum of Art. There are echoes, later, from H.D. and from Gertrude Stein.

Keith Rahmings, *Printouts*
Dan Raphael, *Oops Gotta Go*
Dan Raphael, *The Matter What Is*
Dan Raphael, *Zone du Jour*
Maria Richard, *Secondary Image / Whisper Omega*
Kit Robinson, *Up Early*
Laurie Schneider, *Pieces of Two*
James Sherry, *Lazy Sonnets*
Ron Silliman, *B A R T*
Ron Silliman, *Lit*
Ron Silliman, from *Paradise*
Pete Spence, *Almanak*
Pete Spence, *Elaborate at the Outline*
Diane Ward, *Being Another / Locating in the World*
Craig Watson, *The Asks*
Hannah Weiner, *Nijole's House*

Potes & Poets Press, Inc.
181 Edgemont Avenue
Elmwood CT 06110